CW00921819

Letter to a Muslim Student

ḤASAN AL-BANNĀ

The Islamic Foundation
FOSIS

ISBN 0 86037 258 8

Published by
The Islamic Foundation,
Markfield Dawah Centre,
Ratby Lane, Markfield,
Leicester LE67 9RN
United Kingdom

Quran House,
PO Box 30611,
Nairobi,
Kenya

PMB 3193,
Kano,
Nigeria

FOSIS
38 Mapesbury Road,
London NW2 4JD
United Kingdom

Cover design by Sohail Nakhooda
Cover photograph: © Chris Donaghue, The Oxford Photo Library

Printed by:
Joseph A. Ball (Printers) Limited, Leicester, U.K.

Contents

Foreword

All Praise is due to Allah. May the peace and blessings of Allah be upon His Prophet Muḥammad, his progeny, his Companions and those who follow his guidance until the Day of Judgement.

This short work comprises the English translation of a letter that Imām Ḥasan al-Bannā wrote in 1935 to a student studying abroad in a Western country. Although this letter was written originally to a friend of the Imām for a specific purpose, it contains valuable advice for Muslim youth living in the UK and in the West in general. In view of the enduring message and intrinsic value of this piece it is presented for a wider readership, for all Muslims in the West - students or otherwise. The Imām's sincere *naṣīḥa* (advice) is culled from the life-giving message of the Qur'ān and the *Sunna*.

It is important to note here that whenever Imām Ḥasan al-Bannā speaks of 'your people' in contrast to 'those people', with reference to the people of the Western country, the former stands for Muslims, even if they be of different race, nationality and colour.

We have tried to present the English translation as faithfully as possible to the original Arabic in order to convey the power and spirit of the original without distorting the English idiom.

A journalist once asked the Imām to describe himself. He replied:

I am a traveller seeking the truth, a man searching for the meaning of humanity amongst people, a citizen wishing for his homeland: dignity, freedom, stability, and a good life under Islam. And in resoluteness, I am calling out.

He then recited the following Qur'ānic verses:

> Say: 'Surely my Prayer, all my acts of worship, and my living and my dying are for Allah alone, the Lord of the whole universe.
>
> He has no assistance. Thus have I been bidden, and I am the foremost of those who submit themselves (to Allah) (*al-An'ām* 6: 162-3).

In order to help people appreciate the Imām, the way he understood Islam and the way he practised it, we have added a brief sketch of his biography together with aspects of his *da'wa* experiences, which bring to mind this Qur'ānic verse:

> Of the believers are men who are true to that which they covenanted with Allah. Some of them have paid their vow by death (in battle), and some of them still are waiting; and they have not altered in the least (*al-Aḥzāb* 33: 23).

Included also are a detailed note on the *Ikhwān al-Muslimūn* (the Muslim Brotherhood) organization, founded by the Imām, an English translation of the letter and a Bibliography, listing some English translations of the Imām's works.

We consider it our privilege to bring out this piece of *naṣīḥa*, especially for the benefit of Muslim students pursuing higher education in Western universities. We pray to Allah, *subḥānahū wa ta'ālā*, to enable all of us, in particular the Muslim youth, to surrender ourselves completely to the service of Allah and make Islam a living reality - the dream envisioned by the Imām, towards the realization of which the Islamic Foundation, Leicester (UK) and the Federation of Students Islamic Societies (FOSIS) in the UK have been working over the years in their own modest ways.

I would like to thank Fahad al-Awadi, president of FOSIS, for drawing our attention to the letter of the Imām and submitting its draft translation for joint publication. I am grateful to my colleagues in the Foundation for their generous help to bring out the monograph in the present form. May Allah (swt) reward them all and bless this humble effort with His acceptance and mercy.

September 1995 CE
Rabīʻ al-Thānī 1416 H
The Islamic Foundation

M. Manazir Ahsan
Director General

Life of Imām Ḥasan al-Bannā[1]

His Family

Aḥmad ibn ʻAbd al-Raḥmān al-Bannā, the father of al-Shahīd Ḥasan al-Bannā, worked as a watch-repairer in the southern Egyptian town of al-Maḥmūdiyya. He was also an Islamic scholar who had graduated from Al-Azhar University. He would spend half his day earning his livelihood and the rest in the study and teaching of the Holy Qur'ān and the *Sunna*. He had his own library which consisted of various valuable books on Islam. When the people of the village constructed their own mosque they requested him to become the permanent Imām of the mosque and he duly obliged them. He continued his business of watch-repairing and studied *ḥadīth*, in particular, in his free time.

Aḥmad ibn ʻAbd al-Raḥmān al-Bannā compiled many books on *ḥadīth*. He rearranged Aḥmad ibn Ḥanbal's collection, especially on jurisprudence, and wrote a comprehensive commentary on it.

He wrote explanatory notes on Abū Dāwūd's collection of *ḥadīth* and edited *al-Musnad* of Imām Shāfiʻī (ra), adding a valuable commentary on it. Finally, he compiled a book about the four Imāms.

Shaikh Aḥmad ʻAbd al-Raḥmān al-Bannā had five sons and two daughters from his first wife and a daughter from his second.

His Birth and Education

Imām Ḥasan al-Bannā was the oldest son and was born in al-Maḥmūdiyya in October 1906. The family of Imām al-Bannā was highly educated and well grounded in Islamic knowledge and history. The family followed strictly the Islamic way of life.

The Imām received his primary education from his father who helped him memorize the whole of the Qur'ān at a very young age. He joined the Teachers' Training Centre where he completed a three-year course and came first in the final examination. He then enrolled in Dār al-'Ulūm (presently Cairo University) at the remarkably young age of sixteen. According to the rules he was not eligible but was granted permission on account of his exceptional talent and breadth of knowledge. In 1927 he took his Diploma examination and came first. He then took the job of teacher at a state school in Ismā'īliyya while he was only twenty-one. He lived in Ismā'īliyya until 1933.

His Educational Profession and the Beginning of His Mission

Imām Ḥasan al-Bannā came to Ismā'īliyya in September 1927 on his first assignment. During his free time he studied the social life of Ismā'īliyya in great detail so that he could launch his mission effectively. He endeavoured to become a good teacher as well as a successful preacher. He started his work from restaurants and coffee-houses instead of mosques, and succeeded in attracting a good number of followers within a short space of time. In March 1928, six very important people assembled in his house and swore to live and die for the cause of Islam.

The organization which came into existence at this historic meeting was named *al-Ikhwān al-Muslimūn* (Muslim Brotherhood). The foundation stone of its centre and a mosque was laid in Ismā'īliyya in 1929. Later on, its branches were opened in Ismā'īliyya, the Suez area and Alexandria. Soon this well-planned and organized movement spread rapidly throughout Egypt and later across the world.

Imām Ḥasan al-Bannā had five daughters and one son.

His Works

1. *Mudhakkirāt Al-Da'wa wa'l-Dā'īya* (Memoirs of the Message and the Preacher).

   This diary is in two parts; the first deals with his personal life and the second with the activities of the Muslim Brotherhood.

2. *Rasā'il Al-Imām-Al-Shahīd* (Epistles of Ḥasan al-Bannā).

3. *The Lectures of* Imām Ḥasan al-Bannā.

   Short speeches and religious lectures of Imām Ḥasan al-Bannā.

4. *Maqālāt* Ḥasan al-Bannā (Articles of Ḥasan al-Bannā).

5. *Al-Ma'thūrāt.*

   A collection of supplications *(du'ā').*

(Full publication details of the English translations of these works appear in the Bibliography on p.30.)

His Martyrdom

Imām Ḥasan al-Bannā was martyred on 12 February, 1949 on a main road in the heart of Cairo. He was only forty-three years old.

His Da'wa: Means and Methodology*

In the Coffee-Houses

'I began to think what should be done to remove the friction existing amongst the Muslims. I realized that whoever tried to talk on Islam had to face the reactions of various groups which, in turn, tried to drag him into their own camp, or at least, sought his identification with a particular group. Even if one wanted to establish relations with all the groups and unite them, one would not find favour with them.

I thought on this matter over and over again and came to the conclusion that it was better to keep my distance from all these groups and, as far as possible, refrain from talking with people in mosques. For I felt that it was the people of the mosques who talked about and discussed disputed matters, and whenever they found an opportunity they caused trouble on such issues. Therefore, I decided not to address such people. I thought of other means to contact people for my mission. It struck me, *Why should I not make the coffee-house my target?* This idea continued to strike me for a long time. Finally, I put it into practice. I selected three main coffee-houses that were always crowded with people. I made a programme to deliver two sermons in these three coffee-houses regularly. My way of preaching initially astonished everyone. Soon, however, they became used to it and took great interest.

I took great care in preparing the lectures. I preferred the

* The following account, excluding the note on the *Ikhwān*, is in the Imām's own words.

topics on which I could speak well. I restricted myself to topics relating to Allah, the Day of Judgement, pursuance of virtues and abstention from vices. I did not, in the least, attempt to criticize my listeners nor said anything directly which could hurt their feelings. I simply tried to leave some impressions in the minds of the listeners. I also made my speech simple and used everyday language to suit my purpose. I decorated my speech with examples, anecdotes and other features of public speaking.

Thus I tried my best to attract the hearts and minds of the people and abstained from delivering long lectures that generally put off listeners. The length of my speech never exceeded fifteen minutes. I tried my best to illustrate all the important points of the Holy Qur'ān and *ḥadīth* and briefly explained the main ideas.

The people of Ismā'īliyya liked my approach and they talked about the lectures. They thronged the coffee-houses for this purpose. I also noticed an awakening in the regular listeners. They started to ponder seriously over my advice and suggestions. Gradually, they came so close to my views in that they felt an inner urge to fulfil their obligations to Allah, their faith and to the Muslim community, so that they could attain salvation in the Hereafter. I replied to their questions though in an enigmatic style. I did so to keep their interest alive and let them ponder over the issues confronting them.

In the House of al-Ḥājj Muṣṭafā

We had in mind another house, constructed by al-Ḥājj Muṣṭafā for this gathering. The lovers of Islam assembled there and studied the verses of the Holy Qur'ān. Within a very short time news of the congregation reached far and wide. Generally we delivered these sermons after *Maghrib* and *'Ishā'* prayers when people had assembled there. After this I visited coffee-houses for my sermons.

One night I noticed something disturbing among the listeners. I found them divided into different groups. A question was put to me as soon as I started my lecture: 'What is your view about *Wasīla*?' I replied, 'I think you are not thinking about this issue alone. You will also ask whether the recitation of *Sūra al-Kahf* on Fridays is permissible or not, whether the word "*Sayyidinā*"[2] (Master) be prefixed to the name of the Holy Prophet (saw) or not? What is the position of the parents of the Holy Prophet (saw) after their death and where do they live now? Does the recitation of the Holy Qur'ān reach the dead or not? Whether the present sittings of the Sufis and men of *Sharī'a* should be considered sinful or a means of reaching Allah?' I related almost all the disputed questions that had divided them in the past. The man was stunned by my response. He said, 'Yes, I want to know answers to all these questions.'

I replied, 'My brother, I am not a religious scholar. I am just a teacher. I have learnt some verses of the Holy Qur'ān and *ḥadīth*. I have also studied some Islamic topics and gained some knowledge of Islamic *Sharī'a*. I am preaching Islam voluntarily. If you want me to speak beyond this area, I would not be on sure grounds. If you like my lectures and feel that you have benefited, then pay attention and if you wish to know more, you are free to approach some other scholars. You can obtain opinions on these issues from scholars who are able to help you. Whatever I know, I have placed before you. Allah assigns responsibility to a person according to his capability.'

The man who had put the question to me was very much impressed by my talk and could not find the words with which to reply. I was thus able to avert the trouble and avoid a disturbance. Most of the listeners were satisfied with my explanation. Without losing the opportunity I addressed them:

'My dear brethren, I know very well that the questioner, and most of you, wish to know to which party I belong. You also want to know whether I belong to the party of Shaikh Mūsā or

Shaikh ‘Abd al-Samī‘. (Two leading *‘ulamā’* of the day representing rival theological camps.) This kind of inquiry shall not prove helpful to you at all. You have wasted eight years on party politics and disputes, now you should refrain from it. We have differed on these matters for many centuries yet the differences still exist. Allah likes our mutual love and unity and dislikes dissension and difference among us. I hope you will now swear to Allah to abstain from such destructive discussions. Try to learn the principles of Islam and follow the Holy Qur’ān and the *Sunna*, so that your hearts are purged. Our aim should be to follow the tenets of Islam and not to insist on any particular school of thought. If we have trust and love for one another, we shall be able to express our views in an atmosphere of confidence and understanding. I am sure that you will accept my advice and adhere to it.’

My appeal proved very effective. They agreed a pledge to co-operate with one another in the spread of Islam and avoid issues of dispute. Every individual is free to have his opinion, until Allah Himself decides the matter. After this discussion we continued our preaching peacefully. Now, I made it a point to discuss topics that related to mutual love and co-operation among men of faith. I tried my best to inculcate into them feelings of Islamic brotherhood. Sometimes, I took up issues that were not in dispute among them. I tried to tell them how the pious people of the past exhibited tolerance for others, despite their differences of opinion.

An Illustration

I remember I once cited an example in this connection. I asked them, ‘Who is *Ḥanafī* among you?’ A man got up and came close to me. Then I asked, ‘Who is *Shāfi‘ī*?’ Having heard this question, another man approached me. After this I told the people that these two gentlemen would offer prayers under my Imāmate. Then I questioned, ‘O Ḥanafī: What will be your practice regarding the recitation of *Sūra al-Fātiḥa*?' The *Ḥanafī* replied, 'I shall keep quiet and not recite *al-Fātiḥa*.' Then I asked the *Shāfi'ī*, 'What method will you follow?' He replied, 'Certainly I shall recite *al-Fātiḥa*.' Thereafter I asked, 'O *Shāfi'ī*, what shall be your reaction toward your brother's prayer who is *Ḥanafī*?' He replied, 'His prayer shall be null and void because he did not recite *al-Fātiḥa* side by side with the Imām which is one of the pillars of *Ṣalāt*.' Then I asked the *Ḥanafī* gentleman, 'What is your opinion about your *Shāfi'ī* brother?' He replied, 'He has committed a sin because to recite Sūra *al-Fātiḥa* side by side with the Imām is an act of *Makrūh Taḥrīmī*.'[3] Then I asked both of them, 'Would you try to destroy the beliefs of each other on the grounds of difference?' Both of them replied as with one voice, 'Certainly not!' Then I asked the audience, 'Will you criticize them?' They replied in the negative. Developing my point further, I said, 'Allah be praised, you remain silent over this important issue, regarding the legitimacy or otherwise of prayer, yet you are not ready to tolerate a person praying "*Allāhumma ṣalli 'alā Muḥammadin*"[4] or "*Allāhumma ṣalli 'alā sayyidinā Muḥammadin*".[5] You will make this trivial issue the cause of dispute and a big trouble.' This method of *Da'wa* proved successful. The people started reconsidering their attitude toward one another. They realized Islam was simple and broad-based. There is no monopoly of any individual in Islam. The focal point of Islam is Allah and His Messenger (saw), to be obeyed by the Muslim community and its leaders, if they really exist.'

The Ikhwān (Muslim Brotherhood) Organization

Egypt in the 1920s was a country in deep crisis. Since the 18th century, this traditional Muslim land was subjected to the onslaught of modernity and rapid destructive influence of industrialization and Westernization. Most Muslim countries in this period were under direct colonial rule and Egypt was under British rule. The traditional power structures that upheld Muslim societies for centuries collapsed and the symbol of Muslim unity, the *Khilāfa*, was abolished. Each Muslim country became a separate entity and Muslim societies faced an unprecedented turn of events.

The situation in Egypt in the 1920s was similar to that in most other Muslim countries at that time. The descendants of Muḥammad 'Alī Pāshā were symbolic rulers of Egypt but the *de facto* rulers were the British. The *'Ulamā'* of al-Azhar had lost their influence on the masses owing to the societal changes brought about by modern education and the gradual secularization of all spheres of life. The sufi brotherhoods, renowned for the discipline of their adherents and their complete obedience to their Shaikhs, seemed, unlike other sufi brotherhoods in Central Asia for example, almost unconcerned with the serious changes taking place in Egypt. As to the emerging modern-type groups such as *Jam'īyyat al-Shubbān al-Muslimīn* (Muslim Young Men Society), despite their sincerity and dedication, they were very limited in vision and popularity.

Ḥasan al-Bannā was aware of the strengths and shortcomings of the existing groups. In forming the *Ikhwān* (Muslim

Brotherhood), he tried to adopt their strengths and avoid their weaknesses. The *Ikhwān* was a blend of many elements combined with the charisma and practical genius of Ḥasan al-Bannā. The efficacy of spiritual prowess, discipline and complete obedience to superiors is the most striking element of this organization. One does not have to look far for an explanation for the emphasis on spirituality and deep relationship with God in this organization. This is, in fact, owing to Ḥasan al-Bannā's obvious spiritual inclination, and his early and lasting association with *taṣawwuf* and Sufi brotherhoods (*ṭuruq*). However, al-Bannā also made use of the modern organizational structures adopted by modern groups. At the top echelon of the organization, was al-Bannā himself as the *Murshid al-'Ām* (General Guide), a position which he held until he was assassinated. Next in authority is the *Maktab al-Irshād* (Bureau of Guidance). This Bureau is the legislative and consultative organ of the Muslim Brotherhood, and the number of its members is proportionate to the number of districts contained in the *Ikhwān*'s map of Egypt (12 in the days of Ḥasan al-Bannā, now 14). A representative of each district is attached to a member in the Guidance Bureau, and these different representatives form what is known as *al-Maktab al-Tanfīdhī* (Executive Bureau), whose task is to implement the Muslim Brotherhood's policies. Members of the Guidance Bureau also have other specific duties such as supervizing women or student activities, liaising with other parties and so forth. Each district is divided into several branches (*Shu'ab*, sing. *Shu'ba*) and each branch in turn is divided into small units called *Usar* (sing. *Usra* = family). Each *Usra* contains, ideally, five members.

The *Usra* is thus the basic unit of the *Ikhwān*'s organizational structure and its most important component. It is in this *Usra* that members of the *Ikhwān* receive their spiritual, political, educational and *da'wa* training. It is the ordinary members of this *Usra* that are the real force of the *Ikhwān,* since they will, in principle, grow to become in-charge of *Usra* (*Nuqabā'*), then presidents of *shu'ba*, in-charge of districts, members of the Executive Bureau, members of the Guidance Bureau and finally the *Murshid* of the whole organization who is chosen from amongst the members of *Maktab al-Irshād*. The members of the *Ikhwān* are chosen by recruitment only. After a long period of training and close supervision, an assessment is made whether the person under training is fit to be recruited as a full member of the *Ikhwān* or not. The circle of the *Ikhwān* also contains non-members who are called sympathizers (*Muḥibbīn*, sing. *Muḥibb*). Within the same *Usra* there is an organizational hierarchy which depends on the seniority of the members and other considerations.

Ḥasan al-Bannā's greatest achievement was his ability to create a sophisticated, organizational structure aiming to translate his vision into real life. However, what distinguishes the *Ikhwān* (Muslim Brotherhood) from other groups which were established in the twenties and afterwards is the former's holistic approach. The *Ikhwān* was not merely a social, political or religious association or group. It was described by its antagonists as a state within a state. For not only did Ḥasan al-Bannā create institutions and facilities to cater for the needs of his organization and the ordinary people in society in all domains, he also established a secret élite task force, *al-Jihāz al-Sirrī* (the Secret Organ), to protect his group from any outside danger. Certainly Ḥasan al-Bannā did not believe in the immediate use of force in the process of change. In fact, he believed firmly in gradual change and avoided, as much as he could, confronting the state. However, he also believed that his movement was bound to clash with those who do not believe in Islam as a complete way of life. He was, therefore, prepared for any eventuality that might inflict damage on his organization and its adherents.

The other unique feature of the *Ikhwān*, in its beginning, was that Ḥasan al-Bannā and those who rallied around him did not confine themselves to the traditional venues such as the mosques, to call others to their *da'wa*. Ḥasan al-Bannā began his work in cafés and harbours, in the streets as well as in mosques and clubs. He used to tour the whole country, sitting with ordinary peasants, eating bread and onions with them, and sleeping rough. He did not shy away from going to places where the compassionate Word of God is hardly heard. Scores of prostitutes and drunks repented and became devout Muslims because he visited them. This is a lesson that the Islamists of today may well learn. Intellectuals and students are fine as a target for *da'wa* work, but these are only small components of society. The ordinary person in the street, whether aware of the mercy brought by the Prophet Muḥammad (saw) to mankind or not, is the fertile soil where the seed of *da'wa* ought to be planted.

After the assassination of Ḥasan al-Bannā, the *Ikhwān* appointed a new *Murshid*, Ḥasan al-Huḍaibī. But assuming leadership of the *Ikhwān* at this juncture was not so smooth as it was in the time of al-Bannā. In 1952, Egypt was changed from a monarchy into a Republic by the movement of the Free Army Officers. At first the relationship between the *Ikhwān* and this movement was cordial, since the *Ikhwān* had played a major role in establishing this movement within the Egyptian Army. But, the relationship soon began to deteriorate because of the differences in ideological vocation and policies. Jamāl 'Abd al-Nāṣir deposed Muḥammad Najīb as leader of the Free Army Officers and himself assumed its leadership. Nāṣir, aware of the potential strength of the *Ikhwān*, was determined to either win this organization over to his side or finish it off. And for the first time since its inception, the *Ikhwān* was threatened not only from without but also from within. Ḥasan al-Huḍaibī, in the mind of some leading members of the *Ikhwān*, was not a good choice for the post of leader. 'Abd al-Nāṣir used some of these people in an attempt to occupy the headquarters of the *Ikhwān* and impose a change in its leadership. This attempt failed, and the people responsible were expelled.

The open opposition of the *Ikhwān* to Nāṣir's regime was to prove costly. The leaders of the *Ikhwān* as well as thousands of its members were arrested. Eminent members of the organization were executed in 1954 and Ḥasan al-Huḍaibī was sentenced to life imprisonment due to his ill health. This severe test that the *Ikhwān* faced contributed to the growth of their popularity. Seeing their emerging strength in Egyptian society, 'Abd al-Nāṣir again ordered, in 1965, the arrest of leading figures of the *Ikhwān* as well as thousands of its members. Again, some of them were executed and others sentenced to long periods of imprisonment.

Upon the death of Nāṣir in 1970, Anwar al-Sādāt became President of Egypt. In order to boost his popularity and oppose the growing strength of the leftists, the leaders of the *Ikhwān* as well as its members were released from prison in 1971. Ḥasan al-Huḍaibī died two years later and was replaced by 'Umar al-Tilimsānī. Al-Tilimsānī's leadership was marked by its tolerant approach. He extended the hand of friendship and love to everyone and had a special relationship with the Coptic Church. Al-Tilimsānī died in 1986, and was replaced by Muḥammad Ḥāmid Abū al-Naṣr, one of the senior members of the *Ikhwān*.

AL-BANNĀ'S LETTER TO A MUSLIM STUDENT

My brother in Islam (whom may Allah guard and protect).

I praise Allah for there is no god but Him. May the peace and blessings of Allah be upon Muḥammad, who was sent as a mercy to all of humanity, upon his family, Companions and on all those who hold fast to the *Sharī'ā*, until the Day of Judgement.

May the peace and blessings of Allah be upon you when you travel with a proper intention and a noble purpose, and when you return with a sound endeavour and to a dedicated cause.

May the peace and blessings of Allah be upon you as you serve Islam with the finest fruits of science and the best of knowledge.

Dearest brother, you will be amongst people you have not known before and characters you are not accustomed to. In you they will see the example of a Muslim. So make sure they see in you the best example and the finest image, in order for them to understand that the word 'Muslim' embodies virtue and nobility.

With you is a precious trust, that is your righteous wife, appreciate this. Towards her be a trustworthy companion. Provide her with comfort and happiness. Share with her felicity, without being careless in acquiring your rights and negligent in performing your duties.

Read these few words that are borne out by my love and sincerity for you, as an elder brother expressing for his brother and sister the best wishes and the happiest life.

1. O my brother, excel in your observance of Allah (*swt*) in all your dealings. Understand that He (*swt*) keeps watch over you, sees you and encompasses all that is of concern to you - wherever you are. He knows the treachery of your eyes and all that your heart conceals. Strive not to let Allah (*swt*) see you, except that He is pleased with you.

Do not be unmindful in your observance of the One (glorified and exalted is He), otherwise Satan will infiltrate you and you will be overcome by the whispers of your whims and desires. Believe, my dearest brother, that whenever a heart is conscious of Allah's observance, it will never be approached by Satan. However, once it departs from Allah's awareness, evil will be attracted to it and it will be inhabited by whims and desires. So, consolidate your heart with the observance of Allah and in vigil seek refuge from your surroundings and do not be among the unmindful.

2. Perform the obligatory duties which Allah has enjoined upon you, at their appointed times. Do not neglect them by relying on performing them at a later time, because you are busy with work or resorting to other excuses for justification. This is a deception of your *own self and of your own whims:*

> And follow not desire that it beguile you from the way of Allah (*Ṣād* 38: 26).

Understand also my dearest brother that no one draws nearer to Allah with anything more beloved to Him than performing the obligatory duties as stated in the *ḥadīth* of al-Bukhārī.[6] So be aware not to neglect your obligatory duties or feel lazy in performing them; they are Allah's right over you.

Be steadfast in prayer and perfect your fast. If you are in a state of complete inability to fast, then according to the saying of Allah (*swt*) you have a remission:

> . . . For those who are capable of fasting (but still do not fast) there is a redemption: feeding a needy man for each day missed. Whoever, voluntarily, does more good than is required, will find it is better for him; and that you should fast is better for you, if you only know (*al-Baqara* 2: 184).

But be aware not to take this verse as an excuse for falling short. Fasting with hardship in the homeland of the West will earn you a valuable reward and be an asset to your account; it is pleasing to your Lord and righteous to yourself. So do not attempt to break the fast, unless you are unable to complete it.

I need not advise you, any further, towards your obligatory duties, after all they are your capital. Can you imagine one who has wasted his capital, what will his state be amongst tomorrow's profit makers?

3. Spend whatever time you can in performing supererogatory works as duties of obedience. Perform the *Sunna* prayers. Increase your appeal for forgiveness and the praising of your Glorified Lord. Remember, that one's supplication, during travel or in expatriation,[7] will be answered; hence, increase your supplication in secret and in humility.

Continue your remembrance of Allah (*swt*). The Prophet (*saw*) advised 'Alī (*ra*) to continuously dampen his tongue in the remembrance of Allah.[8] Do not abandon that path which leads you to nothing but duties and obedience, they are like an investment that multiply rewards. The remembrance of Allah amongst the unmindful nations is like a shining light. So make use of this time, for it is a season to harvest the rewards of the Hereafter, only for those who wish to seize the opportunities and benefit from such seasons.

4. Increase your recitation of the Glorious Qur'ān with understanding and deliberation. It is a healing for the soul and a

comfort to the heart. Designate from it a portion to read at the beginning of the day and a portion to read at the end of it, hence the best beginning and the best end.

5. In the delights of life and pleasures of the world, you will see that which inclines the heart, impresses the mind, attracts the eye and bewilders those whose spirits are weak. Do not let these seduce you away from virtue and cause you to forget the Hereafter:

> Do not turn your eyes covetously towards the embellishments of worldly life that We have bestowed upon various kinds of people to test them. But the clean provision bestowed upon you by your Lord is better and more enduring.
>
> Enjoin Prayer on your household, and do keep observing it. We do not ask you for any worldly provision; rather, it is We Who provide you. The ultimate end is for piety (Ṭā Hā 20: 131-2).

Be aware my dearest brother that in the sight of Allah (*swt*) all these pleasures weigh not even the wing of a gnat and lead neither to honour nor virtue. They are nothing but the manifestations of whims and pitfalls of seduction. So be careful not to let Satan deceive you, otherwise you will plunge into the abyss of sin and corruption. Always remember the words of Allah (*swt*):

> Men are naturally tempted by the lure of women, children, treasures of gold and silver, horses of mark, cattle and plantations. These are the enjoyments in the life of this world; but with Allah lies a goodly abode to return to (Āl 'Imrān 3: 14).

The Book of Allah recites these facts day and night. So do not be amongst those who favour the worldly life over the

Hereafter, or amongst those deceived by the outward appearance of things without considering their essence. All pleasures brought by contemporary civilization will result in nothing other than pain. A pain that will overwhelm their enticement and remove their sweetness.

So avoid the worldly aspects of these people; do not let it take over your command and deceive you, if you are to be among the successors.

6. Dearest brother, what Allah has made *Ḥarām* (unlawful) for us, those people consider it as *Ḥalāl* (lawful) for them. Hence, when they commit a *Ḥarām* (unlawful) act, they will neither feel ashamed nor will they refrain from perpetrating it. You should neither agree with their whims nor mix with them in their sins. Otherwise, you will not be relieved from having to answer before Allah (*swt*) and it will not hold as an excuse on the Day of Judgement.

7. Do not take their girls for company, and do not let there develop between you and them, any special friendship or any emotional relationship. If this kind of socializing is a sin for those other than you, then it is a sin twice as great for you - and you know well the meaning of this.

Although you are known to us to be one that is trustworthy and decent, I have mentioned this to you, to caution you against the downfalls of sins so that your feet may never slip. And in your chastity let there be content and in your dignity let there be adequacy.

8. As for alcohol, do not approach it. And do not use the climate as an excuse, because when Allah made it *Ḥarām* (unlawful), He had full knowledge about all types of climate but did not exclude one country from another or one nation from another from this prohibition. Allah (*swt*) made it forbidden with neither doubt nor exception. So be aware not to let it

occupy a part of your abdomen, otherwise it will remain as a black spot on its pure skin.

Be determined as much as possible before the first drink. Because once your mind is concealed by it, you will follow it by the second and third drink, whereby you will have fallen into a pit, difficult to escape from and will have incriminated yourself and others. Then, even if you expiated this sin with repentance, you would still not match your original purity and superb credibility.

9. Do not taste anything in those restaurants which serve *Ḥarām* (unlawful) food, like pork and dead meat. In that which is *Ḥalāl* (lawful) you have a substitute and enough for contentment. So do not taste the *Ḥarām* (unlawful) and do not let your flesh grow on it, otherwise fire is what it deserves. Allah (*swt*) has prohibited that which is impure:

> . . . He enjoins upon them what is good and forbids them what is evil . . . (*al-A'rāf* 7: 157).

So leave that which is bad for that which is good.

10. As for casinos, night-clubs, and other such places of vanity, your time is far too precious to be wasted in them.

I have looked into the saying, 'time is made of gold', and I do not approve of it. Time is far more precious than gold, for time is life. Is it not true that your life is nothing but a few hours and you never know when they will end? Dearest brother, be stringent with your time and do not spend it except in that which is significant, and acquire pleasure in that which is lawful.

In the heavens there is calmness and on the earth there is beauty. In the gardens there is freshness and in you there is a sign. In the sea there is might and in the air there is nourishment. Take from all this comfort for your soul and recovery for your mind. And do not waste your time by being unmindful, this will shield you from good and lead you to evil.

11. Be critical, with insight, and be just and well acquainted with people. Do not let your goodness draw you to forget their bad, and their bad hurt you to forget their goodness. Rather, study them as would a researcher and an examiner.[9]

Encompass with knowledge all of their affairs, and then with an eye of insight, scrutinize it all. Present back the good that you find to your people and nation, and return with it victorious and supported. Other than that, throw it back on them and do not come back until you have dusted off your hands and emptied your mind of it all.

You will find there a group of people dishonouring your Prophet (*saw*), faulting your Qur'ān and disgracing your people. Do not sit with such people, until they turn to a different theme, even if it is necessary for you to enter into a dialogue with them.[10]

Argue with them in the best manner. Explain to them the good that you know and avoid controversies that lead to hatred and sedition (*fitna*).

> Lo! You (O Muḥammad) guide not whom you love, but Allah guides whom He will. And He is best aware of those who walk aright (*al-Qaṣaṣ* 28: 56).

Dearest brother, be aware that calling the people through practical example is far better than calling them through speech.[11] It is far more fruitful and beneficial to use your commendable character, the perfection of yourself and your straight manner to defend and call them to your religion and nation.

Whenever an opportunity arises for you to deliver a speech or a lecture at one of their meeting places or societies, prepare yourself for it. Choose that which will not stir disorder and that which will not offend integrity.[12]

Do not be apprehended by their stance, because Allah's aid is with those who are sincere. Be positive and do not insult other people's beliefs - instead, elucidate to them their innate goodness and reveal to them our beliefs. By doing so, you will have adequately promoted awareness and incentive.

Finally, and there is still so much for me to say and I would have loved to continue this advice with you, yet my concern is that if I prolong this discourse any more, you may forget most of what I have said; for overspeaking does distract one from what is being said.

For both of you then, may Allah raise you to be the best of the successors and may His safety accompany you. May He protect both of you and return you in goodness, as is wished by those who are sincere. I entrust to Allah your religion, your obligations and the outcome of your actions. May the peace and blessings of Allah be upon you. *Āmīn.*

Notes

1. From *Memoirs of Hasan al-Banna Shaheed* [with some editing]. Karachi, International Islamic Publishers, 1981.

2. Master or lord.

3. *Makrūh Taḥrīmī* means an action which is strongly disapproved.

4. May the blessings of Allah be upon Muḥammad.

5. May the blessings of Allah be upon our lord/master Muḥammad.

6. On the authority of Abū Huraira (*ra*), who reports that the Messenger of Allah (*saw*) said: Allah (*swt*) said: 'Whosoever shows enmity to someone devoted to Me, I shall be at war with him. My servant draws not near to Me with anything more loved by Me than the religious duties I have enjoined upon him and My servant continues to draw near to Me with supererogatory works so that I shall love him. When I love him I am his hearing with which he hears, his seeing with which he sees, his hand with which he strikes and his foot with which he walks. Were he to ask [something] of Me, I would surely give it to him, and were he to ask Me for refuge, I would surely grant him it. I do not hesitate about [seizing] the soul of My faithful servant: he hates death and I hate hurting him' (Al-Bukhārī).

7. On the authority of Abū Huraira (*ra*), who reports that the Messenger of Allah (*saw*) said: 'Three kinds of prayers are to be granted without an iota of doubt: the prayer of an oppressed person, the prayer of a traveller and the prayer of a father for his son' (Abū Dāwūd and Tirmidhī).

8. I could not trace that *ḥadīth* which mentions 'Alī ibn Abī Ṭālib (*ra*). However, on the authority of 'Abdullāh ibn Busr (*ra*) it is reported that a man requested the Prophet (*saw*): 'O messenger of Allah. The Islamic edicts appear to me a bit too much, so kindly tell me something (lighter and easier) which I should hold fast to.' He (*saw*) answered: 'Let your tongue remain busy constantly with the remembrance of Allah' (Tirmidhī).

9. On the authority of Abū Huraira (*ra*) who reports that the Prophet of Allah (*saw*) said: 'People are like mines of gold and silver. Those of them who are best before Islam are best in Islam, if they understand; and the spirits are like gathering armies, among those who are similar in qualities, they get mixed up with each other and those who are not, they drift away from each other' (Bukhārī and Muslim).

10. Allah has enjoined upon you in the Book that when you hear the signs of Allah being rejected and scoffed at, you will not sit with them until they engage in some other talk, or else you will become like them. Know well, Allah will gather the hypocrites and the unbelievers in Hell - all together (*al-Nisā'* 4: 140).

11. O you who believe! Why say you that which you do not? It is most hateful in the sight of Allah that you say that which you do not (*al-Ṣaff* 61: 2-3).

12. 'Alī ibn Abī Ṭālib (*ra*) said: 'Speak to the people about that which they can comprehend, otherwise you run the risk of making people disbelieve in God and His Messenger' (Bukhārī).

According to 'Abdullāh ibn Mas'ūd (*ra*) the Messenger of Allah (*saw*) said: 'Whenever you speak to the people of something their mind cannot comprehend, it could lead some of them towards *Fitna* (disbelief or doubt)' (Muslim).

Bibliography

1. *Towards Understanding the Qur'ān*. 5 vols. By Sayyid Abul A'lā Mawdūdī. Leicester, Islamic Foundation, 1988-1995

2. *Riyāḍ al-Ṣālihin*, Vols. 1-2. Compiled by Imām al-Nawawī, translated by S.M. Madni Abbasi. Karachi, International Islamic Publishers, 1986.

3. *Forty Ḥadīth Qudsī*. Selected and translated by Ezzeddin Ibrahim and Denys Johnson-Davies. Damascus, The Holy Koran Publishing House, 1977.

4. *Memoirs of Ḥasan al-Bannā*, Translated by M.N. Shaikh. Karachi, International Islamic Publishers, 1981.

5. *Message for Youth* [Risālat al-Ta'ālīm]. By Hasan al-Banna, translated by Mohammad Najm. Ta-Ha Publishers Ltd., 2nd ed., 1993.

6. *Saḥīḥ Al-Bukhārī*. Translated by Muhammad Muhsin Khan. 9 vols. Riyadh, Maktabat al-Riyadh, 1982.

7. *Five Tracts of Ḥasan al-Bannā (1906-1949): A Selection from the Majmū'at Rasā'il al-Imām al-Shahīd*. Berkeley, University of California Press, 1978. This selection contains: (a) Between Yesterday and Today; (b) To What Do We Summon Mankind?; (c) Towards the Light; (d) Our Mission; (e) On *Jihād*.

8. *What is Our Message?*, By Hasan al-Banna, translated by Aziz Aḥmad Bilyameeni. Islamic Publications Ltd., Lahore, 1974.

9. *The New Renaissance*. By Ḥasan al-Bannā. First published in Kemal Kapat (ed.), *Political and Social Thought in the Contemporary Middle East* (New York: Praeger, 1968). Reprinted in *Islam in Transition: Muslim Perspectives*, eds. John J. Donohue and J.L. Esposito (Oxford University Press, 1982).

10. *Return of the Pharaoh*. By Zainab al-Ghazali, translated by Mokrane Guezzou. The Islamic Foundation, Leicester (UK), 1994 (Also contains a long introduction, describing the efforts of the *Ikhwān al-Muslimūn* in the cause of Islam.)